Pink Goo is about a spiral down to anxiety and depression and the following journey to find peace. After trying to shed light on social injustice, sexual harassment and the climate collapse, the poet finds herself in the darkness and explores many corners within herself, rough and soft. In the deep furrows of her mind, Éloïse finds a white canvas on which she paints with colours to lift her spirit while allowing nuances of grey to tell the depth of reality.

These poems are to aid the reader who wants to scream but doesn't find the words. They are a balm to spread on trauma wounds. They care for the soul after a storm.

All rights reserved
© Éloïse Armary 2022

The rights of Éloïse Armary to be identified as the author of this work has been asserted by her in accordance with Section 77 of the Copyright, Designs and Patent Act 1988.

Cover design by Soofiya
Photo credit Alice Pierre

ISBN: 978-1-7393172-1-8
Ebook ISBN: 978-1-7393172-0-1

Second edition, 2023

PINK GOO

Éloïse Armary

the void of the vase

no one wants to face   the void of the vase
no flower to put in   just air

anyway   the vase is rusty   nobody was there
to feel its texture   love it as it is
keep it shiny

no one wants to smell   the shit and the piss
the sweat and vomit   the morning after alcohol

the movie cuts to the party
the bokeh and the kiss   the beautiful words
the smiling eyes   the loving cheeks

i could write in detail about my hairy ass
i could show hours   of the dirty world

isn't poetry a fine art?

everyone wants to read   about colourful flowers
the shining light showing   the dusty air
that only enhances   the petals' unique texture

how nice they smell   you could almost feel them
rubbing against your face

no one wants to hear   about the void of the vase

halloween is for ghosts

not abusers that i ghosted
you come back

HAUNTING ME

in the shape of another man, texting me

get naked   go to bed   now

i forgot about you   putain   putain

i thought i was lucky   when i read
people of my gender have all known abusers
i thought   nia

shit   this is me, too

ME TOO

worse than that   you came back into my life
you changed your name   but your eyes are the same
your picture is stuck   with me
i use it for some voodoo shit
remember my sanity   when you are gaslighting me

i didn't want to let you win
i didn't want to give you the key   to my mind
so i just completely   shut the door

our story is the opening scene of a horror movie
i see you like tony in london with all your bodies

CHOPPED OFF

thrown in the bins   the bins pile up in here
i wonder if that is why   i could smell your stink
just a normal guy   you see
maybe you're crazy   you think (!)

i need you to believe me
to keep the door open   to keep the movie going
i can't end up   like they are on the screen
i won't let him win   but

FUCK

me too

hear their shout

they were crying for help, but i did   nothing
i was too busy with my empty bank account my timetable filled up until it overflowed with sleep, i am late on a monday morning all this noise still leaves space in my ears to hear their shout

I SHOULD HAVE LISTENED

except that next to me people are paid to hear, yet they didn't tune in don't make me feel guilty about keeping up on that tiny bark when you are lying on your golden ship, you say if nothing happens is because people don't care enough,   but

I CARE, I CARE

except if i feel it in my heart or bring it to the streets, i don't see the change, only my exhaustion, i just want to rest knowing everyone around me can sleep in a warm bed cos it freezes me to know people are dying while i am dreaming,   yet

YOU HAVE NO PROBLEM SLEEPING AT NIGHT

your bloody hands tucked under your self-satisfied smile, you make me lose my voice you make me wanna puke my words when you say "People with no papers are the problem to our society. They take all your pennies!" while when you open the paper you see where the billions go:

ON YOUR BLOODY GOLDEN SHIP

all there is left to sleep at night is to hold our own, kae tempest said it all, give our prayers to a god i don't believe in hoping that love will spread
for everyone to find a warm bed

a land that was once free

we are scared, anxious, angry
of our houses destroyed
because of the sea level rising
no fish in the water only plastic
that ugly commodity killed
creatures more beautiful than we will ever be
they were orange, blue and even neon green
but we only see in black and white

collapse means falling without flight
sequoias are wrapped in tin foil
we shed tears with hands in broken earth
no one can share the grief like the earth can

we are scared anxious angry
to be brought up in a world
where every dream is deadly
we are asked what job we want to do when the future is nothing but poverty

jobs that pay are the most useless
and we kill the back of those who hold the spine of our society
we are told to thrive in an upside-down world
when gravity always pulls our feet down to the ground

we are scared anxious angry
when some of us can't afford to live on a land that was once free
we are scared anxious angry
to barely survive in a dying world for a dream that wasn't even ours

two years later

two years later
the same fear   of a year cancelled
yet time goes on
we wake up every morning   a little more tired

two years later
we are exhausted
we never see the light   at the end of the tunnel

two years later
key workers and students   in hospitals, schools, bars, restaurants
                                    music venues, theatres and cinemas
we are all crawling
on a burning ground, moreover

two years later
amazon netflix spotify and deliveroo are flying
spitting their carbon dioxide in our mouths
we swallow it like cum, looking for the last bits of art to chew from
looking for the sweet taste in the blow of a cigarette smoke

help me

looking at the clouds   shapes of dinosaurs and ice creams
smelling the freshly cut grass   sunshine on my face
tasting like chlorine   in a dress showing my panties

like i did without knowing what life would be like
two years later

how to eat leeks under capitalism

i was in bed for weeks
i could only buy leeks
if i smiled at people when serving them theirs
they would hand me a couple of tips
now i'm smiling
but i can't buy these bloody leeks

stop asking me to go here and there
meet friends, enjoy spring and enjoy life

and and and and and and and and and and and and and and and and
and

when i have a tenner on me
yet all day i am

doing doing doing doing doing doing doing doing doing doing doing
doing

making films podcasts writing

this and and that and and and and that and this this this and and that
that

it doesn't pay for my leeks

i hope one day it will

what is a success story?

our sense of success
was to be top of the class
from day one to the last

in maths french and german
regardless of our interest
in any subject

learn to stay on top of the ladder
know where we stand:
above the other classes

we were ranked from top to worse
our essays - not us (?)
we would come home
have only numbers to hold   for our parents to be proud

the future plays on tiny wooden desks and overused pens
we were writing our destiny

do you have what it takes to squeeze in the elite
guard its doors since to enter in, it took your sanity
there must have been a reason
behind years of insomnia and anxiety

other perspectives are scary

if the golden citadel is a lie, what is a success story?

when the sun shines on my pale cheeks

the sun sleeps at 4 pm i wake up at 11 am
we have a 5-hour relationship

but today is for   the dance of clouds in the shape of a ship
the sun and i   barely have time for coffee

i read on social media

                the British sun is like a fridge's light

we are tomatoes   now pale and wrinkled
only our red-ish feature reminds us of summer

we wouldn't appreciate
fresh tomatoes   basilic and mozzarella
their colours   wouldn't feel so bright   their taste   wouldn't be so strong
without months of grey and brown

still   i want to feel
the sea   and its birds
the wind against my coat   my body all wrapped up
in warm woolly layers   except for my hands   i always lose my gloves

instead   i am waiting for a brighter day   i only go outside

when the sun shines   on my pale cheeks
i stand there   on the streets
                                        close my eyes

hoping to be a red tomato   again

"hey, you're alright?"

my glasses are dirty
i vapour them up   clean them with my sweater
it isn't soft like a cotton T-shirt   they stay dirty
they fall off my nose
when I take them off   my vision is blurry
when I look at the camera to take pictures
the screen is blurry   i don't know if the focus is on
i put my glasses back on   keep fixing them on my nose
i need my dirty glasses that keep falling

my hair is greasy
but I only washed it two days ago   i hate washing
i feel cold when I come out of the shower   soggy when I put my clothes on
i don't like my haircut
i made it hastily in the bathroom   with my broken scissors
i had too much hair   it wouldn't dry properly

i   just   had   to   cut   half   off

the line is uneven   i didn't care
i do now that I am standing at a party   with uneven greasy hair
i have this birthday hat on   to celebrate at the party   I look ridiculous
with my tiny hat on my uneven greasy hair my dirty glasses that keep falling

if that was it i could enjoy my time but the dog is screeching in my left ear
the balloon is popping in my right ear the music is - is that glass animals?
the bathroom tap is on
you are talking too low for me to hear clearly I am so drained by everything
i am talking lower than you are saying to me - sorry what was that?
i apologise and repeat but all i want to do is

have a shower and stand in a quiet field
my skull is scratchy   my pubes are stuck in my knickers
i do a subtle move to release them   they get stuck on the other side
my side has a spot on - is that from a spider or a cat flea?
i feel it on my breast too   i want to

scratch everywhere and shave my head scratch everywhere and shave my head spread aloe vera all over spread aloe vera all over spread aloe vera all over
roll in the grass and stare at the sun roll in the glass and stare at the sun

"i'm fine - a bit tired. how are you?"

get a dildo

get a dildo
suck dat clit
tip tip tip
are u even attracted to guys
watch porn
no, don't watch it piss and shit
pay for feminist porn
money money money
are you even sexual at all
suck my dick
i want to put it in your pussy
cum cum cum
are you even ???
sorry i don't feel sexy
sorry i'm not dressing hot
sorry i don't make the first move
sorry i turn down yours
i am not even in my body
i only feel the suffering
clenched jaws that taste like wasabi
i only reach under my panties
to cum in seconds
veins filled with alcohol
relax it all
giving you pleasure
or receiving yours
bodies with bodies

you give me brush strokes
i give you photocopies
all i can think about is
chores
put my soul back in my
body first make me feel
nursed
pull the pieces back together
make me feel like a feather

pink goo

i am not very good   at existing
my life is a big jelly   made of all the tasks   from my to-do list
that run into each other   inside a pink goo

i wish it was clear   like an ice cube
i would live inside   a blue ikea fish frame
  i would settle   in the peaceful and quiet freezer

i live in between the fridge and the coffee table

i don't know where my head is   that kid takes a bit of me
leaves the rest in the fridge   comes back
picks the rest   takes bites from the bowl
the candle on the coffee table makes me hot   i sweat a bit
they leave the rest of me   put me back in the fridge
i'm cold again

in the fridge i'm dreaming   of my life in the peaceful freezer
but no one eats icy jelly   i have to take my dreams as reality
try to relax   my eyes closed   embrace that i will never live
in the freezer   only between the fridge   and the coffee table

maybe hippies never existed

my dad told me   uni   would be the best years of my life
full of friends   parties drugs (he did not say that)
i imagined myself   a hippie   in the 60s
half-psychedelics   half-revolution
i did not anticipate   the depression
the work as a waitress or babysitter
instead of chasing   parties
i found myself chasing pennies
i found myself   a student
dreams   not yet crushed
sex drugs n rock n roll
on a fixed routine
same bedtime
everyday
before
my
 mental health
slips away, maybe
i was longing for my twenties
            (after being a student)
when your labour is paid (finally), but that's when
                    dreams get crushed, isn't it

maybe hippies never existed

my thoughts are made of grey

it's hard to see the darkness within myself. acknowledge it. accept it is mine. let it go away. see the racist thoughts in my brain. observe them. say they're there. they are part of me but not who i am.

it's hard to see the ugliness within myself, who can i point inside my brain. something that is mine. i can say that is society inside me. make it a stranger. it is too familiar to say it's another than myself.

settle in the discomfort of being the oppressor.

learn the history of colonialism.

see my ancestors as settlers.

let the shame wash me from the blood and shit of the past.

keep going. keep working. write a better future.

it's hard to talk about race with other white people, they would say the only truth is that there is no race. see colour and you are racist. how often didn't i see someone beyond the colour of their skin even if it was for good. unlike my thoughts i labeled them as different. other than me.

it's hard. to see beyond black and white. accept my own darkness. that while

the world is colourful, my thoughts are made of grey.

i am not a true artist

your art is made of all shapes and colours found in nature
your voice sounds like the river struck by stones of anxiety
they get released as you speak to me
 i'm flowing like a fish in your voice, going wherever you bring me

when i'm swimming in your shapes and your colours i only see my reflection through the water

i cannot get out

i see my own art, still by the shore
from the reflection through the water
the fields are green and the sky is blue   my art is grey
not one of these masterful charcoal drawings like Da Vinci draws elbows

it is a pencil doodle made in class when i was painfully bored of the teacher and had no one to talk to

my art is me talking to myself because i had no one to talk to

i didn't even think it was art   it was just my way of coping
all i had was these grey pencils but I can't even draw
i got so used to paint laying behind a wall of glass i couldn't go through watching "true artists" making art   being destined to watch on my seat

on my fucking uncomfortable seat   behind this wall of glass

all i wanted was to run   see all the shapes in nature
in the mountains and in Budapest   so I did

when i ran i found places with paint   just there   in front of me
i could even swim in them if i wanted to
we are all swimming in the paint together

you chose pink i found yellow   we drew tulips and the sun

when you create from nature i create from my mind

i dig in my mind   alone
sometimes i get confused
the shapes i create, inspired by my grey pencil doodles when i had no one to talk too does not mean i am alone now

 i am not alone now

i'm flowing like a fish in the river of your art
you're jumping on my brain doodles

we are together, making art

Soof & Aloo

you are kind and fluffy
soothing and soft
and all the words that make you fizzy
on the skin and on the spine

you figured it out
how to craft your space
in the midst of a time
where it's hard to fit in
you found your home in images
bright colours and soft letters

Aloo is like hibou genou doudou
like that song that my mum sung to me
to learn the French words that end in X
but there is no X in you
X is hard under the tongue
X is for the plural

you are Soof & Aloo, singular
you are as soothing
as this song my mum sung to me

when i see you, hear you, read you
i feel that there is a space in this world
for me to carve out
made of love and smiles and zines
for me to create
despite these hecking bills

there is a space for love
soft and soothing
all the words
that make you breathe   bigger and longer
that make you smell the fresh air of this world
there is a space for everyone   to thrive in

some call it a happy place
i call it
Soof & Aloo

i load the first film in my camera

i load the first film in my camera
i wear a green coat and a purple checkered shirt

so 70s

my mum would say
with her laugh

BORN IN 1969

when The Beatles played on that roof
i type this on the latest iphone
i never recorded hours and hours and hours and hours and hours
on film   cut with scissors
i just use audition   or premiere pro
i wish i wasn't so slow
my style is just play-pretend   fake authenticity
a vague fantasy of a time

I REALLY FANCY

i probably wouldn't be there as a woman
holding a camera   hosting a podcast   making videos   who knows

I AM BORN IN 2000

i wear brown trousers and an orange jumper
i load the first film in my camera   in 2021

i don't know anything about astrology or watching the moon

covid rises
like mercury retrogrades
i want to write a stars poem
but I don't know anything about astrology

my boredom grows
in parallel with the moon
shall i just watch it pass
but i walk too fast
people tell me
"are you in a rush?"
"no, I just grew up in paris where walking slow meant no oxygen, loud smells and a meltdown"

i could slow my pace down
smell the air
the morning wet grass
be there when the moon falls asleep
but I don't know anything about watching the moon

people who say putain

my little bit of france
the images you have been fed of a dream country
tour eiffel   bérêt   baguette
none of that   ok, yes   baguette

my memories instead   colorful snapshots
of laughter and pain   crêpes   jeux de mots   putain

this is why i traveled   maybe it's all the same
i don't want french   to be the water i swim in   monolithic grey
i want   to stand on the sand   dip in the blue

observe its colors from far away   close enough
i can see my own reflection   my body shape   moving
at the rhythm of the waves   words all over my skin
i am wearing a story

i thought there would be a bit more laughter abroad
but don't attack my pain   cos it is mine

my france   and your france   won't ever be the same
who am i kidding   see, i talk about my france   in english
but my words will probably be read by people who say

putain

maybe home isn't where i expected it to be

women together
in a room
from different countries
cultures and religions
we will break
your expectations

different accents
different words
same language

different skin
different hair
same beauty

different ages
different stories
same emotions

different smiles
different laughter
same joy

i cannot go to my homeland   cross a tiny sea
yet we are around the same table
when our feet have travelled   from far away oceans

strange familiarity, women together in a room
maybe home isn't where i expected it to be

bipolar is not a tragedy

bipolar is not a tragedy no
no
this is not hamlet
we won't seek your tears your - that's terrible what a horrible life
we're tapping into your fears
that bipolar is all around you
promise, we won't attack you
it's not all nurses and drugs
in a four-wall white bedroom outside your city
bipolar is in my home
there are tears, oui
but the eyes above them
i deeply care about
and haven't you ever cried?
we have laughs
we have loves
we have dreams
you don't know the ending
because bipolar is not a tragedy

thoughts are fishes in the sea

everyday on wikipedia
anxiety
depression
ADHD
autism
bipolar
type I
type II
typed once
typed twice
my fingers
frenetically
looking
for a label
to stick
on a box
to throw
my thoughts in
no box fits
thoughts still
swimming
like a soggy sock
that lost their partner
they feel out of
place and keep grieving

through my nostrils
the breath remains
like waves that rock my thoughts
they can let go and float
on the water's surface
relax the heart relax the shoulders
relax the knees relax the toes
thoughts are fishes in the sea
whatever name we want to give them
they belong in the water
none bad none to extinguish
my thoughts are drifting to the shore
where my body lays
on the rocky beach
they found a home
in dirt and algae

like two rabbits

we stay up
lay in the night
cosy in bed
wrapped up in warm sheets
you reading
me saying silly things
in love
like two rabbits
in a mud hole
i kiss your arm
and you my forehead
on my leg
a tiny little rabbit
all black on black sheets
nature made him so dark
so that any picture would look terrible
so i put my phone down
look at his tiny face
happy like a monk
i delay the moment
i will fall asleep
unconscious
in the void
dreams i can not control
waiting for me
my muscles relaxing

one
by
one
the warmth of my body
the beast shaking in his own dreams
i have hours of rest
below me
i don't want to stumble in it
i want to dance around
delay
delay
delay
until
like an act
i bow
to conclude the day
rested before i rest

Glossary of poems

the void of the vase	5
halloween is for ghosts	6
hear their shout	8
a land that was once free	10
two years later	12
how to eat leeks under capitalism	13
what is a success story?	14
when the sun shines on my pale cheeks	15
"hey, you're alright?"	17
get a dildo	19
pink goo	21
maybe hippies have never existed	22
my thoughts are made of grey	23
i am not a true artist	24
Soof & Aloo	26
i loaded the first film in my camera	28
i don't know anything about astrology or watching the moon	30
people who say putain	31
maybe home isn't where i expected it to be	32
bipolar is not a tragedy	34
thoughts are fishes in the sea	35
like two rabbits	37

Thank you

Pauline, for filling the home library with stories to get lost in
Charlotte, for taking my hand in seeing hard truths
Tom, for making me write love poems in English
LAC friends, for creating space to read poems out loud
Mum, for encouraging me to keep on my literary exercises
Alice, for reading each other's writing with such care
AFLO the poet, for leading me to stumble upon the poetry scene in Brighton
Ella & Ollie, for my first open mic at Words by the Water
Dad, for being vulnerable with me
Ellie, AFLO the poet, Ella, Heather, One Inky Queer, Ali, Simon, Pete, Gracie, Charlotte and Kimberly, for our conversations on Poetry to your Ears
Nuria & Monica, for printing my poem on beautiful paper
Reanna, for giving so much
Soofiya, for your softness
Heather, for holding each other's hand through this mad journey
Tom, for everything, there is too much to thank for

Poets from the past, for the stories you passed down
Poets from the present, for making this life sweeter
Poets from the future, for pouring your heart out to strangers

Reader, for trusting my words

Éloïse Armary (she/they) is a French poet and filmmaker based in Brighton, UK. She is the co-host of the podcast Poetry To Your Ears and director of the documentary film Collections Of Queer Poets. Éloïse writes poetry to make sense of her mind and the way her body moves through this world. She writes from a queer, neurodivergent and multicultural lens.

@eloisearmary / www.eloise.armary.com

www.ingramcontent.com/pod-product-compliance
Lightning Source LLC
Chambersburg PA
CBHW042130100526
44587CB00026B/4251